The Game Is Played on a Delicate Foundation

and even better poems

George Arthur Lareau

SUFI GEORGE BOOKS
TUCSON

Copyright 1962-2007 by George Arthur Lareau. All rights reserved under International and Pan-American Copyright Conventions. No part of this work may be reproduced or transmitted in any form by any means, electronic or mechanical, including photocopying and recording, or by an information storage or retrieval system, except as may be expressly permitted by the 1976 Copyright Act or in writing by the publisher.

ISBN 1-885570-37-6

Sufi George Books: http://sgbooks.sufigeorge.net

Publisher's Notice

This book includes:

THE HUNTING POISE Copyright ©1962, 1989 by George A. Lareau. First published in 1962 by the poet in a limited edition of 200 copies. LCCCN 62-19718. The title has been taken from an untitled poem by Lawrence Ferlinghetti, contained in his volume, *A Coney Island of the Mind.*

READINGS AT THE BOILING POINT Copyright ©1967, 1989 by George A. Lareau. *Readings at the Boiling Point* is a collection of poems most of which were first made public at a reading by the poet at The Boiling Point, a beatnik-style coffeehouse, in Freeport, Illinois. First published in 1967 by the poet.

THE GAME IS PLAYED ON A DELICATE FOUNDATION Copyright ©1994, 2002 by George A. Lareau. Published by Sufi George Books, Phoenix, Arizona U.S.A.

Several more recent poems are also included.

Table of Contents

Publisher's Notice 3
Introduction 9
Elder Oak 11
indian summer 12
interim 14
Rockport 15
Pan 16
lo, the valley and the brook 17
morning 18
Dream of War 19
Yesterday 20
aging 21
winter 22
art mechanism 23
this room 24
Next Time 25
perspective 26
only the silent wind 27
for the moment 28
reverie on a spider 29
a poem for new year's eve like 30
Ode to the Toad 32
To Myself, In College 33
monkey man 35
smoke-filled room 36
the alley 37
Suite 203 38
woman in maze, walking 39
from dream awakened 40
bowery 41
Kol Nidrei 42
escape 44

wanderer	45
Part One	46
autobiography	47
the hunting poise	48
Aphasia	49
Shock Wave	50
The 4 Yogas	51
Helen: An Encounter	53
Let Us Dine	55
Astronaut	56
Automation	57
The Four-and-one-half Bell	58
One For the Road	59
Moon	61
Churchmouse	62
Presumption	63
Wander	64
Yer Hair	65
Plea	66
Cheers	67
Naked Whore	68
A Message for Janene	69
Many Miracles	70
Where Is a Mountain?	71
In a Cathedral	72
Reply	73
Romping	74
To Sweet for Chaucer	75
A Point	76
Commodity	77
Cash Value: $1	78
The Romance of the 500 Cigarettes	79
Vision	81
Zonk	82
And Things Like That	84
Destruction	85

A Party	86
On the First Night of Christmas	87
Jane-Jane	88
That Rowboat Feeling	89
This Little Boy	90
Cry	91
Poem of the Age	92
Pressure of Despair	93
Head	94
The Creation	95
Hollow	97
Something to Say	98
Circles	99
Here Is a Man	100
Poppets	101
Don Quixote	102
the days of love	103
alien	104
The Game Is Played on a Delicate Foundation	105
Tastes and Touches	106
Shimmer	108
Together	109
One Moment One Day	110
My Motive	111
You Are Enough	112
Wanna Play Ball	114
Duty Do	115
The Mayor Conducts a Council Meeting	116
Prisoner	118
Words	120
The Story of Cindy	121
The Urge to Write	126
With Eyelids Closed	127
Recognizing You	129
Poetry Doesn't Pay	130
Ants	131

Jack on the Mountain	132
A Face In the Clouds	133
Sandwich	134
Donna Lena	135
Donna	136
For My Beloved Rebecca	137
The WP Blues	139
Create	140
Done It All	141
Zorba's Dance	142
Mother Goose Took a Shit	143

Introduction

George Arthur Lareau was a very bad college student. I was a very bad college instructor who allowed him to receive academic credit in philosophy for minimal perusal of some of the so-called "great minds."

It was rather evident in the spring of 1959 that Lareau should be given an opportunity to cultivate his own poetic visions rather than be forced to learn about intellectual systems. Even my driest pedantry was not concerned with Lareau's traditional education, for he read voraciously and observed and reacted to things and people in a unique manner.

Lareau's poetic vision is extremely broad and fortunately cannot be labeled as belonging to any one school or tradition. The careless reader might relegate Lareau to the "angry camp," or to the mystical tradition, or dismiss him as one of many American nature poets. All of these epithets are conceivably helpful in finding some frame of poetic reference within which to appreciate Lareau's poetry.

However, if one were narrow enough to take a preconceived label and affix it to Mr. Lareau's poetry, the result might be of conversational interest, but Lareau's poetic stance would be farther away from the reader than ever.

Mr. Lareau is concerned with whatever strikes him as excruciatingly and personally real. His reality may not be the same as that found in scientific textbooks or in treatises on sociology or religion. Whether Lareau writes of prostitutes, snow, city streets, or forests, he seems to affirm that man's greatest value, rather than mere rationality and scientific progress, is the ability to see significance in little things of the moment.

Although Lareau speaks to us on a personal level about personal things and experiences, he is well aware of the limitations of popular humanism. Paradoxically, he suggests that man can only find his self-identity through escaping his own ego.

Spending his life in the loneliest places--the city and the country--Lareau's poetry is greatly concerned with man's alienation from nature.

Lareau has the characteristic of isolating unexpected phenomena and constructing unknown worlds before the reader's eyes. Much of Lareau's imagery is of a physical and sensuous nature, yet it is endowed with a sense of the dream-like and is indicative of a strenuous search for values no matter where they may be found. Lareau appears to say that the feelings and creativity of individual people can elevate the human status.

Some of Lareau's poems abound with social satire and commentary, yet there is never any indication of the poet spitting in the face of his fellow man. He shows only a weary empathy for mankind and speaks in a tone of inner quietude.

Phillip Caddell Kennedy
May, 1962
The Encantada
West Crafton, Redlands, California

Elder Oak

Good morning, elder oak!

We keep our private rendezvous
at never-hour

Tonight we are not lost in
early morning's black envelope,
for the illumination of the snow
reveals us,
and exposes our love scene

Yet we embrace courageously,
displayed for seeing eyes

I kiss your rough bark skin
and tremble under the maternal
protection of your branches

Our love is seen by the
snow-sheet's light

indian summer

as the indian summer breezed
the blossoms rained an
aromatic shower
willow's tears tumbled
to the ground, caressing
the pasture grass
underneath the storming beauty
beckoned two hazel eyes--
I was sucked toward them
trees began floating dizzily
squirrels ceased their
conversations,

the music I heard braked
to a sea-gull tempo,
and I responded:
what filled abysses were those eyes!
how they had no end!
they surrounded me with their
encompassing projection
they seemed to grasp and pull me
until I was cushioned and massaged
by the thunderingly silent storm
by her side

how pink a blossom lullabyed
between us, stirring the air

with motions soothing as the
waving of the field behind us
but, overwhelmed together,
I saw released a tear, another,
sparkling with sadness
once before had she been here
and left;
she had to leave again

as she explained, I understood
that she appeared in season,
and had the need to gather life
each time that she expired it
even as I sat there, she faded,
for beauty was she seen as
and the indian summer breeze fell
to the leaves, entered the branches

interim

naked willow, winter tree,
a blemish accompanies
your scream of death
(hear the speech from
blemishes such as these
as the barren willow
branch sleeps)

recessant zeal of
active hibernation
climbs to the tips of
leaf-pores,
when leaves flourish,
yet, that is for a moment
for winter trees, leafless,
shadow the heart as a statue

Rockport

endless stones
surrounding me,
and there, the ocean
as a speck, an interruption
in a natural setting--
I am there
trespassing in a world
not claiming me as
a natural complement
and I am sickened
and embarrassed
at my existence

Pan

a forlorn foghorn
breaks the distance
surrounding me in
ecstatic euphony
i am absorbed into
the overwhelming calm
where the seagull dips
at the crest of the wave
there am i the focal point
i burst with joy
then relax with a
bewildered
pleasured smile

lo, the valley and the brook

rush the waters through their paths
with frenzied haste to mute restivity
in union with the sentry's leaves,
fallen to a journey in these seas

lo, the valley and the brook:
they travel in benign satisfaction
no destiny, no awareness of fatality--
only peace pervades in this season

night is still, and crickets sing
satisfied reflections of the day

morning

morning sounds in
silences

last evening's
crickets, quieted
the melodies of birds
are petrified

all is captured in a
frozen nuance
to be absorbed by
saturated morning ears
asleep

Dream of War

The world stopped and the word was:
There's going to be a war
a war like never before
soon too
ils pleurs plus fort dehors

The signs were right, perfect,
and very obvious to the
trained astrological eye

And Nostradamus said it too
but no one remembers
and it is good that they
do not remember

For there I was, eating
a steak-this-thick, when all of a...
yes, it is good that they chose
not to remember

I remembered, and there I was
cowered in the corner between
three mountains, protected,
...but waiting

I was one of the heavy rain-drops
that fell before the storm began

Yesterday

let us talk of
yesterday,
of the ocean voyages,
and the stalls
at Mardi Gras
of yesterday,
with colored costumes
and people shouting
in crowded streets

yesterday, --who
sees the dreams as
vividly as we;
we, forced to dream,
sitting in our
rocking chairs
let us smoke a
pipe full
and reminisce

aging

the realisis descended:
in a rapid backward motion,
memory focused between
the parallels of youth and
manhood, closed a door,
and forced the gaze to
revert to the volumes of
the unsuspected future.

startled, trembling,
the infant flounders
in his thoughts. with fear
noting the vast circumference
of the marvel at hand
he questions initiative,
searches to avoid surrender,
offers that he did not choose
to be released.

winter

stumble-bumming winterside
slope into the rushes,
swallow the dehydrated gorges,
make a rabbit
die

craze the hedges,
saturate autumn leaf-piles
wreak your pleasures
on the three sisters
you've never met,
and forget...

art mechanism

the strange ones leer
at the darkness; the
strenuous search once
conducted provided no
comprehension

the foggy shuttling
the figments of acrid
odors, the fragmentary
counterpoint; these all
appeared illusory

yet they stopped to
capture on their canvasses
and trap in meter
this subtler illusion

this room

this is how i got in this room
with no windows and no doors:
i was born here

they say i must die in this room
with no windows and no doors
i cannot leave this room
they also say

it is a strange question to them
leave? to go where?

outside, i answer
but they say to me, this room
has no windows and no doors

but i want to go outside

Next Time

It was in diminishing rays
last time

Sol was vertical to our
horizontal bodies
His arms were mighty at the
shoulder and they tapered
to the top and to the bottom

This time it is Plaloc's
nourishing manna--
we are sheltered by
the glistening sheet
of his rain-drops
suspended from a roof's edge
slowly slipping
and it is a warm rain

Next time it will be
another season
our expanding appetite
will tide us far beyond
the crystal, wet or dry
we will devour the salting
of the moon

perspective

into the myriad sun-filled clouds
wandered an eagle, as, on the shore
my love and i embraced

the waves thundered only ten feet
below us, and our feeble elevation
was enthralling

between the resounding blindness
and the silent magnificence, we,
reduced to audible sounds and
controllable movements, belittled
to the majesty of the entire planet
before us, began weeping

in the detachment that ensued
we together studied the water
constant and untiring in its
attack upon the rocks
making progress only over
hundreds of years, and we said
we have not that much time!
we have not that much time!

only the silent wind

only the silent wind
and its power
propel us

the rippling water
moistens a background
for our exercise on love

with ripples the water
is disturbed
and from the stars
we gather our emotion

for the moment

weep later, cry tomorrow,
tonight we must forget

no remembrances can undercurrent
our sensations, for this
is a moment we must struggle
to revive, we are alive!

there can be no time,
nor, for the present,
reflections of discomfort

no fears: this moment
is of our creation, let
us not surrender
to thinking of reaction
for we as a faction
in melodious desire,
we are afire

reverie on a spider

never will I entertain
a spider in my house again;
a spider spinning webbed snares
which hold me powerless to gain
my winged freedom as a fly--
no spider is a god for I!

a poem for new year's eve like

what this bongo 45 rpm pachanga
like Puerto Rico
here I come!

silences interspersed....
(this stanza is about the old year,
which fades, quickly-quickly)
the old year fades quickly-quickly,
and the thermometer shudders
unaware of passing time
fluctuating temperatures
it wishes they'd fluctuate
a little less frequently
it was born in the Arctic

(this stanza is about the new year,
which approaches quickly-quickly)
the new year approaches (void)
ha fooled you and the calendar
is about to embark on the famed
Metrecal diet, but it will not stop
but will eventually diminish in
weight until it has vanished
into pure nothingness
and a memory

the calendar is like the
Thanksgiving turkey about

four weeks before Thanksgiving
It just doesn't know what
is going to hap-pen.
Neither do you....

(Note: this poems contains
all of the ingredients belonging
in a poem designed to usher in
the new year: truth, idiom,
extremely humorless humor,
rhymelessness, toilet paper,
and the new secret ingredient
for the year, which, of course,
is still secret)

Ode to the Toad

of humble creatures
the world is filled
with ugly ones too

the toad is a specimen
of an ugliness burden
a curse of the gods

how worthy of ode
is the swallowing toad
flies, mosquitoes and other insects

To Myself, In College

Run little boy, run away from it all
when there seems to be too much—run

To the movies tonight, to the bar
tomorrow night
--or maybe the bar after the movies
tonight, and somewhere else tomorrow
Run little boy, run.

It's not worth it: listen to that
It's not worth all that needs to be
put into it. That's not part of
your goal
not part of your plans
So run, little boy, run. Run away.

Say this to yourself:
Say that it is nicer outside;
say that it is really the pleasure
of the moment that is important
that you shouldn't live in the future
forever. Don't come inside,
little boy,
run.

After all, didn't you do well in the
play?

Didn't that show you off?
So now, you can run, little boy--run away.

And several times this year, haven't
you shown spurts of real colors?
They'll remember your colors,
don't you think?
They'll understand if you
run away now, little boy.
So run, little boy, run--run away.

Chicken-ass bastard little boy!

monkey man

two years ago my monkey die.

I stand on street corner
and street side turning crank
on hurdy-gurdy music machine
with smile on my face, beeg smile,
and wait for people to drop money
in little tambourine

two years ago my monkey die,
and now I am monkey.

smoke-filled room

smoke-filled room(boom)orchestra
satirizing(bobby doop oop oop)
men-wimmen, wimmen-men oopy-
dooping, the constant struggle
(bidop a doobiddy wham; boom)

Christ! goes the fight, foolish,
converted into frivolity, ridiculed,
senseless(waaah)? Tears soak the
human soul, bitter and rebellious
hazing everything in sight, and
Itself

(whee hee la la la)the clarinet
laughs: the god in the music
free from the body, from life,
from being born, being dead,
being limited--ah, limitations!--
(except the air on which the notes
do travel)bom, bom, alas, bom-m-m,
no freedom

the alley

darkly steps are climbing
the walls, and faintly a
lamp is speaking--dimmed
is the quietude, yet my
awareness is keen toward
an age-ridden resonance
which lingers there, and
permeates my being, as I
stop in the alley to
absorb the essence of erosion

Suite 203

typewriter jungle--
office animals beating
their rhythms on live keys,
but making dead words,
errors,
and abbreviations(abbv.)

office animals living for
coffee-breaks
Fridays
payday-heydays
and more jungle clothing
porcupine haircuts
turned-up collars
(marks of distinction)

for birds of a feather
amass together,
and fall to the hard ground
seemingly without injury
(insensitivity to pain)
the devil may care

woman in maze, walking

one awkward leg advances
then the other--she climbs
down the narrow cobblestone
maze-way

around this corner
she cannot attack what she
might expect to find there

bolstering her courage
she strains in effort to
swing her heavy legs

her anxiety mounting
she frets as the corner
approaches her

alas! this corner is
another cobble-stone maze-way
which leads to a corner....

she continues, unprepared
to conquer what she might expect

from dream awakened

my dream is ended,
for in it i was free

bowery

women tear at their
ragged dresses
despairing the uselessness
of their bodies

and old broken men
stand on street-corners
waiting for some
stimulating passer-by
to give them an erection

and i crying out to them
saying to them Be calm
i suffer enough for all of you

to no avail, for
they inform me
i am one of them

Kol Nidrei

[written as a translation of the musical impressions of Kol Nidrei, Bruch, for violin and orchestra]

Orchestra:
I cannot see beyond my fear,
my liege; vision fails me
in this hour, and bares me
prey to my unawares

Violin:
Though you tremble and think
you fear, be calmed:
the ocean in its turmoil
has yet to find its understanding
and a tree that for a hundred
years is mute, it bears its fruit
To its own music, deaf is the lute

Orchestra:
Yet, must I, who am possessed
with flesh and shimmering
intellect, be as these?
Where is my power?
How it fails me in this hour!

Violin:
Merry float the summer winds,
tossing loosely with the leaves--

revels are their happy occupation--
watch you then these children
and learn their fascination
Delight to daytime is found
only in the night

Orchestra:
It is your desire then, to see
me afire with identity of
all of nature's wealth?

Violin:
I have no desire, for
in simplicity one can find
the golden harmony
A field is silent, yet is
nourished to maturity

Orchestra:
With my hundred ears I hear
and receive a hundred thoughts
how I fail to assort them,
how I fail!

Violin:
Stealth in thought is
focus in the eye;
far above the voracious
monster, you can see the puppet
and watch his passions
form that cloud

escape

my god is fog,
my encompassing protector;

he shields me from the
stinging rays and bolts

i am propelled in a sea
in which odd fish stare
seeing only the turbulence
revolving around me
and they do not care

great shield,
reject me from your heaven
of nebulous sensation,
and return me to the horror
of naked individuality!

wanderer

wanderer, the roads are long
grant yourself a resting spot
enter in the gates of question

noble is your search tonight

expectations make you meals
you can feast with due delight!

wander through a misty valley
wonder at the sightless eye

fear destruction at the hand
of accidental tyrannies--

gaze then into the fog
and look for God

Part One

I have labored long, Unknown,
constructing slowly a road
by which you might come to me

Praise me for my fasting
for my suffering has become
as second-nature to me
and I rejoice in my devotion

These decades have been longer
than many lives, and
I have grown an old man

Stay your eye gentle on me,
for it has been a trying labor
searching your illumination

and in these last moments
I fear fatigue may overtake me

autobiography

the cycle of neutrality
composes all my incidence--
i wince

i dwell in surreality
floating on the picked fence--
a trance

screams for materiality!
the echoing sounds thickly dense;
rose lens

the hunting poise

an arrow, slithe from rooted bow,
flies as a dangerous boomerang

the hunter jumps, avoids its
stinging attack upon his feet,
and so it goes, leaping
up into a spiral hell

takes out his fangs, gnaws
the forest's edges; strange
the centermost tree should topple
sparing few around it, so it goes,
a chain-like series finally wresting
from the hunter's grip his weapon

curious the tears smiting elbows
with their heated bodies--this,
this is the hunter's poise

Aphasia

and are they strange things
floating around in my skull
in the middle of interrupted
nights and are they foreign
are they not mine, and are they
not mine and are they
not mine?

i hear a jazz piano in the
night staccato dark foreign
what is a night without a
hot sound like dark foreign
night hot big piano big
um face big big jazz um floor

big books read them and all
resolutions big answers and
strange answers foreign
big dark hot sound like and
questions with staccato answers
and questions and questions

Shock Wave

Plunk is a rain
and a happy noise--

fertile green of a storm
in a wind-blown hill,

gibberish in a bird talk
and a happy noise.

a quiet sound startles
a sleepy-sounding bee

and we awaken
to a happy noise

The 4 Yogas

aw, be scintillating,
be jubilant and exciting,
be refreshing and inspiring
be sharp

tell me some keen mystery
about life and why it happens
and about me which is really
something that makes the birds
chirp in the morning

hey, i got an idea
let's see who's more real
between the two of us
there ought to be one just a
little more real than the other
huh?

i'll bet you one thing
i'll bet you that i'm the
only one of me

but maybe there's another
come to think of it

i saw two snowflakes one day
they fell in my eyes at the
same time and i saw them
because they were the same

as each other which i thought
was a refreshing bit of learning

lordy, you're just sitting there
whatsa matter, you got an itchy
ring finger or something?
i mean rings and crosses are
okay for some people but i always
thought you were made of pretty
real existent-type stuff

Helen: An Encounter

from the swiftly ruptured heart
flow complexities of blood ephemeral
horribly redder than before

tiddly-winks and bottomless beer:
i know we could have lived well
together but in the course of
human events

the time for the equal reaction
has come and i tremble to suffer
the blasting whatever it will be
whatever

how will food be swallowed
tomorrow reminding me of the
body which in spite of
tumultuous deprivation of
terror's appetite remains
oblivious?

feet will wear shoes tomorrow,
won't know change of pace
increased weight, duty,
walking, won't know

how can the conflicts not see
each other not make warfare
simply do their treacherous

duty simply existing simply
exist side by side

how can the ruptured heart
contend with the aspirations
of a head so complete with
profound filosofee how can
the ruptured heart?

toast the english, scrambled eggs
continues ringing in my ears
oblivious to the ruptured heart

Let Us Dine

come let us dine in our thickened peasant stew
with our ears filled of songs sung in tripoli
our eyes with each other engaged in reverie
and a blossom revived watered well as if it grew
in an empty skippy jar

surrounded by bolero in a constant melody
of transcendence above our routine monotony
come let us dine at our multi-leveled board
and inspect the treasures of the cornucopia's hoard
we dislodge the unseen bar

Astronaut

We lost an astronaut today
Today we lost an astronaut
The astronaut today we lost
Today an astronaut we lost
And nevermore another shot

An astronaut today we lot
Tolot we day an astronaut
The astroday tonot we lay
Tolost an astrosnot we say
Another shot more ever and

Automation

on the auspicious occasion blah blah blah
we are happy to announce the removal
of a hope from the life of a frammy
walla boom doom is his new perspective

we regret that happiness could not be
suffa guffaw now done most efficiently
by automation which will zing flaw

allowing for a certain period of time for
adjustment
by removal of the human element it has
gluck strang the production of which
will insure the greater safety and
comfort of a nation of unfeeling people

The Four-and-one-half Bell

and even the town of Boston closes down
and has its dead hour from four to five
except for a few all-night cafeterias which
do no trade and a few stragglers like
myself wandering around and walking in
a thoroughfare with arms up high and
feeling the sensation of the freedom
of the power and with no one watching
releasing a giant sigh

the four-and-one-half bell sounds
and all is well

One For the Road

There's a little blinking blue light
which is telling me of cheer
it is spelling out a new sight
by a brewery of beer
it says blue beer is so cheery
and that cheer beer is so new
and that near bear is so bleary
and that clear beer always sneers
and green beer is dear
and stale is frail
and warm like your foot
in the fireplace
that's real beer taste

I like whiskey it is frisky
brisky drink for winter tricks
trisky trinkets make my whisky
blackest of the crisky thinks
thinksy I that mint or whisky
is okay for building bricks
or for carpentry in winter
is the summit of my licks
and the streetlight of my kicks
the serpent of my dreams
on the blackest winter night
who turned on the lights

that sweet tavern of mine
the floors are full of slime

does it make you puke?
just look at that juke
Box it twinkles my knees
if you please, and I do

Moon

in spite of the traffic, the sirens,
the streetlights, in spite of the
turmoil
the yellow river moon
behind a cloud, the connecticut
river moon, bathing in its
aura, enjoys a conversation
of the moon between itself
in the mississippi river

Churchmouse

like a churchmouse,
whose quiet world is weekly
blown to shadows with
gigantic music and
growing oratory,
so am i from time to time
reminded of my purpose

Presumption

feeling my way along
what I presume is a railing
in what I presume to be a void
of black cavernous tunnel,
I stumble for a moment,
presumably on a log,
and I scream a tentative
call for help.

Wander

alas, my brother has found a
home and wanders about no
longer--we travelled a long
and strange road together and
he has become the stronger

and now i find i am walking
alone to satisfy my hunger
and am bewildered
and prone to linger

Yer Hair

so yer heve got to heve dis feelin
like wen yer goes ta dry yer
hair wen yer washes it
an it slops on yer forehead like
thet makes yer feel like yer eyes
ain't much good wit da hair in em
yer see

or wen da wind is blowin
yer hair in yer eyes an
yer could cuss it wen yer hair
is in yer eyes

or wen yer goes ta water
yer garden in a dry spell and da
wind blows dust in yer eyes
an on top of it blows yer hair
in yer eyes an yer could cuss
da wind, yer could cuss da wind
or da water or da dust but
yer never cusses yer hair

Plea

my plea
is always: come with me

i never hear
but only speak this plea

it tumbles from my tongue
like a mantra
constantly rolling
dulled with use.

but sometimes you hear it
as a fresh new song,
and you come with me

with you we can rescue
fallen leaves by
stopping the seasons

Cheers

Let us have some cheer!
(with a ho ho ho)
Christmas time is here;
quickly! some (commercial) cheer!

It is time to be gay (how absurd
among the many is that word!)
with a ho ho ho

The prescribed mood is jolly:
Haste: be blind and succumb
to this manifested folly
and on a hearty note
go ho ho ho

Naked Whore

now it comes the naked whore
in blemished black ferocity
a trauma strange and billowy
a trauma light and bilious
a trauma sillyous

comes at once in bleakened emphasis
sudden in its tragic pale
sudden in its gross demeanor
sudden in its apathy
its blackened smashedy
ghostly in its snapethy
ghastly sillyous

A Message for Janene

Your mother called--
she said there is no love left.
She said when you come home
to bring some bread

Your mother called,
and said she has no feelings--
she asked if you would please
forget that bread.

Your mother called,
to say that she is lonely.
She doesn't want you there--
just send the bread.

Many Miracles

of the many miracles
that i have never seen
and the several talks with God
which i have never had,
and the few times there has been
an unseen glimpse of heaven,
i think the thing that i like best
is when i never wakened

Where Is a Mountain?

where is a mountain?

i am befuddled by this
very flat, serene nonsense.

from here i can see
all of the world i know
end to end

and over there is distance

where is a mountain?

from here i can see
over the heads of the
tallest people in these parts.

the tallest buildings aren't too tall
and i see over them

measuring the flatland beyond them
to the end of the end

where is a mountain?

must i look up
to see a mountain growing?

In a Cathedral

oh look the little hut where jesus lives
with god & the priests monkey around
& sneak in there sometimes i bet!

& how quiet like i should woopee
& run down the aisle & trip on the
chancel & play marbles with my teeth

hey! let's paint a mustache on that
statue--oh, it's a woman! well, let's
draw something different on her then

new game--i'll climb up these stairs
& you climb up those & we'll see who
reaches the preaching platform first!

i win! i get to sermonize! oh, here's
some notes, how handy--is everybody
listening to me? is everybody ready?

Reply

give me your crying
and i will give you tears--

for your heartache
i will give you pain

but to your love
i will reply with love

Romping

fair wonder in landish
abstruse is the singeth
and melodies chiming
a peal of ripe cheer

in season are blossoms
of mirthy blue bonnets
and eateth my collar
of obtuse hue clear

but noose is a grackle
and buds on the lamp
so cleary is bleary
you scamp

To Sweet for Chaucer

a child's melodye
is bland and usually monotonye
but must contain a certain qualitye
because so many find it charming, too cute for
words, but generally I disagrye.

A Point

Creation is a
relatively insignificant act
when you consider
all the damned confusion
that results.

Commodity

They trade daily in the market
of powers--some of the bargains
aren't too good, according to rumor,
but the trading is active today.

Generally speaking, there's an
atmosphere of great affairs about
it all--sort of a lesson in how to
be big by acting big and kind of
spending the little simply important

field-full of pennies marching at
orders and calmly agreeing about
trading: here a life, there a life,
everywhere a life life.

Cash Value: $1

you see the stage and on it is a stranger
behind it stranger things and people
there is some light to amplify discerning
seats also sidelines at a stable

you hear a question asking your commitment
but weakly and if you're not careful
the questions fail to mark your soul intruder
relentless questioning continues

are you the man from whom we gather manna
the lady filtering our sorrow
you are the child demanding our surrender?
you think not for it is yourself there

The Romance of the 500 Cigarettes

I tell you now about my romance which
lasted until the fire died and I could
light no more cigarettes but in the
darkness of a warehouse listened to the
mice in the ceiling and sometimes to
one that fell into a wall somewhere

We are old men now, you and I, nodding
our heads in the warmth of a bubbling pot
or riding in the subway standing reading
over someone's shoulder; there's no war
time was when cheering on the streets
filled our thoughts and we remembered
fighting filled with wondrous sounds
marvelous showers of light; speed;
ah, yes, and before that we were real men--

but was that really us standing there?
it kind of looks like a picture,
doesn't it? one of those pictures
newsmen take and put in papers,
not of us, but of mr. american soldier.
ah, ah...we get lost. where was I?
the all-night vigil, yes! smoking on
a wrinkled cigarette. what did he say?

i remember it now. i'm going out there
to die. why don't you take my butts.

there's some rotten garbage in this show.

Vision

Yes, I can see it all very clearly now--
You are somebody's child.
Yes, that's not too difficult to see.

Zonk

hey the world is full of it
but the world just goes zonk
instead of warbling about
neat things like existence

now let's just take existence
for example

between you and me there's just
me

you see things cockeyed
but that's better than going
zonk
and falling asleep
like a machine
which is a pretty zonky thing

ever look at a frog?
why?
i mean it ain't nothing
that you should take seriously
it's just one of god's jokes
and a pretty funny one if
you see what i mean

there's this frog going gronk
which rhymes with zonk

which means it isn't real

but me, i sit rejoicing
me, i go unzonk all day
until i've been up for two days
then i sleep, but i don't go
zonk

And Things Like That

the shade is cool, the food is fine
guests number seven, total of nine
the water is fresh like wet lettuce
and drinking lemonade makes the grade
as well as beer and things like that

the women are plentiful, sleep like mink
the swamp is forty miles away
the smell is filtered and made sweet
the sandy beach massages my feet
and my back and things like that

Destruction

how carefully built is
my sandcastle--
how carefully designed,
considered, deliberated,
how great a reward
is my achievement,
and how thorough is
the crumbling destruction

my cozy nest of leaves,
a comfort carefully made,
leaves carried from across
the field, and arranged in
a luscious, inviting pile--
i sleep but once:
and strain my muscles
to accomplish its
destruction

A Party

champagne, see fire flow

the evening is in five rooms
and several speak of squares
multi-colors and later

in and out of two hundred
dollars worth of bottles
people are flowing
quarter to quarter and
vague corporatory background

privacy shared among
seventy? no, thirty, and
it is much better, tonight

let us sit in that corner,
and discuss later, chere,
let us discuss later.

On the First Night of Christmas

and i slept to clear my
head of the alcoholic strain
and to regain
my short-recessed virility

she lay waiting under me
so comfortably covered
with the body of a little stranger

an unknown child too far gone
to play the sacred game

Jane-Jane

Did I think of you?

Did I think of croaking craggies
making whimpers for the flies?
And of flashing eyes of many darknesses?

Did I think of supple berries
of canoes afloat in caverns of
a dizzying ministry?

Of sentle angles probing for
the miser in the woods?

Did I think of willow branches
drifting darkly, falling falling?
Did I think of you?

You're goddamned right I did.

That Rowboat Feeling

feel as the row-boat
maneuvered by man and
by currents doubly controlled

yet feels the illusion of
self-control for it cannot
establish its proper source
of power and assumes
(as aided by conceit)
that it has power and
perhaps it has

(one floated down a stream
once, while only a short
while before it had been
secured to a little dock)

This Little Boy

they who age, ferreted into their legs immobile
carrying arms alongside and upon occasion
touching some object, perhaps a tea cup;

fastened into a purse their lips crackle
when a child backs away from the
compulsive kiss of habit

they who age: where did the new people come
from?

ah, they were not watching, and with a
whimper
they try to command the enigmatic expiration
of
the ever constant continuum to their
understanding--only the contradiction is
obvious--

and yet there is a promise, but conditions
have been explained and not been met.

"Which is this little boy, which is he--
Jean qui pleur ou Jean qui rit?"
--Tennessee Williams

the bulb will soon fuse, but the sun will not
lose its momentum, nor the moon its
persuasion.

Cry

I cry in darkness
knowledge evades me
I cannot hear my cry

Poem of the Age

i am a poet of the age--
progressing toward unknown ambiguities

how can i twist and scorn
the morning sun? let's see.

my poem is of the age--
how can i screw up the horizon
in a stanza indented seven times?

so boleslavski says hey creature
see that tree?
and he says it nice and plain
but he isn't talking nice and plain
at all
let us consider that tree of the age
photosynthetically

but what the hell that tree
has been through it all
and can see through the microscope
without even bothering the lenses

comes and goes, comes and goes
in an age when the rose really ain't
in an age when the poet really can't
him don't dare

Pressure of Despair

the weight and pressure
of the sky
now rests upon my head
it seems it always has

where am i that
when my face is skyward
turned, my nose feel pressed?

time has been when
vibrantly filled with
power i could blow
the clouds in flight

now it is night

Head

There's a certain rhythm pounding--
pounding in my eyes, resounding
in my ears and lightly clowning
with the way I walk. and talk.

Funny things become so funnier--
laughing til it hurts. the crummier
is the joke I get the laughier
and my stomach hurts. and burps.

Everything I see is bouncy--
bouncy to my eyes, renouncy
to my sight and deftly fleecy
as images catch up. and up.

Rhythm to my speech is catchy--
halting after phrases, splotchy
fragments musing on a scratchy
theme til sense is lost. what frost.

Phony gone and care deserted--
inhibition's lost, I'm girded
with a mask to truth alerted
in all that I can see. I'm free!

The Creation

out of the substanceless of nothingness
created hee hee

and one day the very neutral nothingness
the very arbitrarily neutral nothingness
became a positive nothingness
and a negative nothingness
because it didn't really make any difference

and then the positive nothingness looked
around one day
and with the neutral nothingness as its eyes
it looked and beheld the negative nothingness
and said well what is this thing all about?

and since we are practically neighbors
and it is kind of lonely around here
let's have a party: we can sit on this
neutral nothingness and talk
it won't really care very much

and then the negative nothingness heard
this soundless voice coming out of
the edges of the neutral nothingness
and it listened with the neutral nothingness
as its ears and heard an invitation
something about having a party or something

and then the negative nothingness looked

around a little to see what was going on
it just stood there for a little while
and looked at the positive nothingness
and said well what do you know here i was
all alone and didn't even know it how about
that boy you learn something every day

and then the positive nothingness waved his
hand which was actually only the neutral
nothingness which didn't really care
whether it was waved or not

and the negative nothingness waved his
hand back which was only the neutral
nothingness which didn't realize that here
it was waving at both ends and didn't know
whether it was waving at itself or what
but it didn't really care very much about
that sort of thing anyways

and then the acknowledgement of each other's
existence was completed and the negative
nothingness decided that he would answer
a question which he assumed came from the
positive nothingness even if it did sound
like it came from the neutral nothingness

but it was obvious to the negative
nothingness that the neutral nothingness
really couldn't be bothered less about
talking or not talking or things like

that you know what i mean, anyways, the
negative nothingness said well i guess
that a party isn't such a bad idea at
that but i can't think of anything worse.

Hollow

he's no blind man!
he's just empty inside,
that's all

he's vacuous, doesn't
give a hoot about
saying hello or
begging your health or
loving the sun or
waving goodbye or
pointing to birds or
watching the wind or
praising a child or
kissing a flower

he loves himself,
that's all

Something to Say

I have a little something to say.

It's a simple little something
but I haven't found the words
to make it get said
so that it's all said
and not just suggested instead.

I have a little something to say
that words alone won't convey.

Circles

Ignorant Man Happy
Thinking Man Sad
Wise Man Happy

Here Is a Man

Here is a man
he is going to die
he doesn't know why

Here is a man
walking through life
with brogans and boots
and thick overcoats

Nothing can touch him
Except the air he breathes
And it's going to kill him.

Poppets

Who are the goony poppets
all over my back,
like telling "ME"
What I oughter and oughter notter
skribble
ON MY OWN DAMN PAPER!

Maybe they're "ME"
on a little tiny invisible string
that i can't even SEE!

Don Quixote

my vigorous assault upon
the thwarting rules for ignorance,

and I am caught but knowingly
and sent in whirls
as is the pattern of longevity
but not unknowingly am I

and those around me,
marking time
until they die

the days of love

on the first day of blue love
my new love gave to me
eight winning glances
and a poke aimed at my
dead flower

on the second day of cruel love
my stewed love gave to me
some magic potion
to repair my delicacy

on the third day of fool love
my crude love gave to me
one golden chance
to sit still and forget my dreams

on the fourth day of feud love
my nude love gave to me
nineteen refusals
and a song filled with ribaldry

alien

maybe you think my life has been
a very long lark--

you think i've never had
a moment of sad news
even a moment
of sober reflection
only a steady stream
of glorious mania--

wake up:
i'm human, too
i feel as alien as you do

The Game Is Played on a Delicate Foundation

The game is played on a delicate foundation.

The game consists of achieving survival and
and considering matters gravely and
and understanding social phenomena and
and merging with another person and
and these all together are the game that
when desperately enough played
hides loneliness.

The foundation is loneliness.

Loneliness is when that person goes and
and there ain't no mail today and
and the alarm didn't go off yet and
and all together somehow the game stops.

And the game stops.
And the game stops.

and loneliness happens and

Tastes and Touches

I am left with a headful of memories--
curious situation--

what I was after was tastes and touches

tastes that would madden my tongue
and give the roof of my mouth that crazy itch
and make me suck hard
and bury my nose in
and gasp for air between frantic connections

touches that would balance the giving,
would flesh out the giving with response,
would complete the circle of giving
and responding and giving and
responding and unite in a circle
spinning and wheeling and reeling

all that did happen--

but then it became memories
the memories stretch and spring,
they entangle with each other,
they become more delicious than
the events they are depicting,
they become hollow and empty,
they come and go,
they don't obey so good,

they add up wrong sometimes

in the last analysis
the memories must be real--
they're all that's left,
all that endures,
all that contributes to
all that receives contributions

Shimmer

My eyes will not shimmer
or glimmer no more
Your eyes will observe
I don't shimmer no more

Your eyes will stop shimmering
because mine stop glimmering
and our eyes won't shimmer
or glimmer no more

All shimmering and glimmering
will melt into memories,
into doubts of our memories
and wondering if

And wondering if
there ever was really
any shimmering and glimmering
which now ain't no more

My eyes will be shimmerless
and glimmerless all over;
your eyes will observe and
react with dull pain

Your eyes will be glimmerless
and shimmerless and dull
and we will be wondering if

Together

You're right there and I'm right here
and yet we are not together,
we're afraid to be together,
afraid we might be seen together.

Yet we want to be together,
we know that we belong together,
it feels right when we are together,
but we don't dare to be together.

One Moment One Day

we had us a moment one moment one day.

bright sunshine was showing
to us who was knowing
that shadows were stowing
our moment away.

we fell in that shadow one moment one day,

for darkness was speaking
to us who was weakening,
yet light rays were sneaking
to light our foray.

we found us amazing one moment one day,

illumined and flaming--
no longer defaming—
as one person claiming
one moment one day.

My Motive

I've got a motive that's simply swell,
what the hell, the motive is mine,
and you can't see it, so there.

Why do I do what I do, ask you--
fooey, why do you ask like you do?

Now you see it, now you don't,
and maybe you'll see it again, so there.

Right now you can't see it
(my motive, that is)
but it's clear that it's there,
right where you can't stare at it,
and it's making me do what I do.

You Are Enough

I look at your eyes and
they are kind of bulgy;

I look at your nose and
it is bigger on one side;

I look at your chin and
it has a mole with hairs,
I haven't exactly counted
how many hairs grow there.

The part in your hair
has dandruff down the middle;

I look at your ankles and
they are full of insect bites;

I look at your feet and
they are dirty and ugly;

I look at your hands and
they are oversize and rough;

I look at your clothing and
it is bulky and sloppy;

I look at your teeth and
they are crooked and

the edges are jagged.

I look at your ears and
they are small and funny;

I look at your legs and
they are large and fat;

but when it is dark and
I can't see you very well,
and your hair is clean and soft,
and I smell your breath and
your sweet sweat, you are enough.

Wanna Play Ball

Why don't you wanna play
what I wanna play
when all I wanna do
is play ball?

I wanna play ball
with you, wanna play!

Wanna play! Wanna play!
Wanna play ball! Play ball!

You don't have no better idea,
just don't wanna play ball.

You don't have no idea at all,
just don't wanna play ball.

Why don't you wanna play
what I wanna play
when all I wanna do
is play ball?

Duty Do

Do your stupid duty, stupid,
churn earth like a worm.

One day you'll be through;
until then, duty do.

duty-do, duty-do, duty-do.
Turn and turn and turn.

Round you go, out the door.
Duty-do, duty-do, duty-do.

The Mayor Conducts a Council Meeting

Dearly Beloved, we are gathered here
in the company of God and his men
to serve the City with our talents,
with our time and with our hearts.

Yes, Mr. Councilman, you wish to
perform? Very well, the audience
is now yours, and although they
didn't buy a ticket to see your show,
they are equally as captive, so go.

Madam Councilwoman, I believe you
perceive here an opportunity to
play the game, just like the biggies.
Please take your turn, and share
with us your assorted naivetes.

You have the floor, Mr. Councilman,
and now you can be every bit as
important as the real councilmen
of days of yore. Speak--just say
anything, and it will count for you.

What are you doing here, Mr. Councilman, when you would rather be at
home watching TV? Why isn't your
attention on the discussion? It's

too bad you are so uncomfortable.

Madam Councilwoman, there is a smaller
faction represented in your speech;
let me ask you--if the greatest good
is for the greatest number, what kind
of good do you wish for a lesser number?

You are so dispassionate, Mr. Council-
man, in your analysis of the problem,
and yet the solution you propose seems
admirably apt. You are to be congra-
tulated on your problem-solving abilities.

Dear brothers and sisters: There are
around us a number of citizens who have
named us to represent and serve them.
What? There. Right there behind you,
next to that chair there's one, and...

Prisoner

When I was free, before my capture;
yes, there was such a time
though people look at me and think
that I have always been behind these bars;
when I was free I simply
took it all for granted.

I even complained some,
about fending.

I am fed only once a day,
always the same fare,
and some water to drink.
I try to exercise, but
there is very little space here,
behind these bars,and I cannot get
the exercise which I never
thought about before.

I even complained some,
about distances.

It used to be that I could choose
where to defecate and urinate.
Today, I simply do it on the floor,
and from time to time the floor
is cleaned, sort of.

Before I was caged, this freedom
seemed so natural, inalienable.
I even complained some,
about dirt.

I had a companion, one I chose.
Now I am alone, a prisoner,
isolated in an artificial world.
If only I could look at another
like me, even a stranger.

This was once a part of nature.
I even complained some,
about chatter.

Being a prisoner
makes me want things.

Words

Only homely words to use.

the painter only greasy oils,
a sketcher dirty charcoal dust,
the sculptor only rocks and tools,
and only mud the potter has,
to capture beauty, give it breath,
and I to capture you have words.

Homely words, a poor disguise
when draped upon you, for they melt
into your pores and there you are,
radiant with the paint of words,
bursting through the film of speech,
revealed without a need for cloak,
ephemeral made manifest.

The Story of Cindy

Our Cindy's a gal from El Paso,
whose marriage was ten percent hassle.
And eighty percent
Was designed to prevent
The last ten percent being facile.

Reconsidering being a virgin,
Cindy disallowed sexual mergin'.
With her purity regained,
Sex by here was disdained.
In her thought that she's virgin, she's splurgin'.

Our Cindy attracted a lover;
Her heart begged to be handed over.
She resisted a little
And got caught in the middle.
Where she's at now she'd love to discover.

She loves a good gothic romance;
And she likes to imagine the chance
That a lover will seize her,
Will kiss her and squeeze her,
If he'll vanish with no second glance.

A commitment is Cindy's intention
And to give it, she has an invention:
When she makes the commitment,
She will know that what it meant
Is as changeable as comprehension.

Our Cindy, her husband a bother,
Decided that she'd love another.
But when she decided
To chew what she bited,
She flew off instead to her mother.

Our Cindy decided her son
Was a nuisance, she'd rather have none.
But her sister had previously
Dumped her kids; and so, grievously,
Our Cindy missed out on the fun.

While down in El Paso, she rented
A place where her lover, she hinted,
Could see her in private.
Might just nine-to-five it,
Or screw her til he was demented.

For Cindy, the world has its rules;
Disobeying, she says, is for fools.
But she finds it convenient
To be somewhat lenient
On occasions when rules are bad tools.

Cindy thinks that she knows right from wrong,
And she's put it all down in a song.
"Right is right, is not wrong,
Wrong is wrong," goes the song,
"If I'm wrong, I'll be right before long!"

Little Cindy is anxious to please,
But with her it is like a disease.
For she'll please herself never,
Always pleasing whomever
Is her father, by fact or degrees.

Cindy thinks there is time without end,
Time to wait, time to waste, time to spend.
But her secret disaster
Is that each day goes faster,
Bring closer each day her dead-end.

In documents, Cindy has faith,
Whether marriage, divorce or a death.
And it is none other
That makes her a mother
Than the document of Isaac's birth.

Cindy's really a lopsided creature,
And her guilt is her dominant feature.
That she's God's creation
Gives her pure consternation,
And a pure wicked grin to her teacher.

Preparing herself for a journey,
Cindy learned how to make a man horny.
But no book could teach her
The art he beseeched her
To practice upon this long journey.

With her lover, she rode far in order
To see the great falls past the border.
A honeymoon short,
It was just for sport
For she loved him no more than she orter.

Cindy daringly swallowed some drink,
To release her true self in a blink.
Of that moment she thinks
That two daiquiri drinks
Are much fewer than most people think.

Cindy tried very hard to be sexual,
And had learned to be somewhat effectual.
But when all was laid bare,
Nestled there in the hair
Was an organ she'd not made erectual.

Cindy practiced her swearing a little
And progressed up to cursing with "Fiddle!"
Although she ran amuck
Learning to say "fuck,"
She explored some this act in her middle.

Cindy's airplane was far from the border
But her story was good and in order.
She thereupon bent
To her task heaven-sent,
Then went home, and confessed end of quarter.

Cindy knows what she wants, so she made
Her own bed and upon it she's laid.
And she tells her sore heart,
While her lover's apart,
"We all know that the price must be paid."

And she wonders if paying this price
Will perhaps make her parents turn nice;
Or will this new gambit
Bring out love no damn bit,
But just be one more roll of the dice.

On her list is her own happiness,
On the back is her son's scribbled mess.
When the mess grips her mind
She's unable to find

Happiness, happiness, happiness.

Her lover awaits in El Paso,
And Cindy awaits in El Paso,
And the longer they wait,
To become mate and mate,
The more days go by in El Paso.

In an El Paso mountain abode,
Her lover retraces the road
That led him to love,
Then gave him a shove
That changed him from prince into toad.

On the peak of El Paso's great hill,
Is a wandering lover seen still.
A mournful beast,
He gazes east
Through the blur of two eyes with tears full.

The Urge to Write

I notice that the urge to write
comes only when I'm at a loss,
when things seem dead,
when I can't see ahead,
when my life is dull,
when I feel I have no friends.

Then come the words,
rescuing my moments from death,
urging more of my deeper self
to come out and play,
to amuse me and console me,
to give my life meaning,
to help out a poor soul.

Yet they seem only words,
a bare connection with the world,
words no one wants to read,
words that spill carelessly
upon my pages.

A poor substitute for loving arms,
for sweet kisses, warm caresses,
for strokes and murmurs
of loving appreciation.
Only words for friends.

With Eyelids Closed

I've closed my eyes and
my attention is wandering.

I do not notice what
fields it is wandering in,
whether flowers grow there
or whether animals graze.

My attention entertains itself
and I am not aware of it.
Yet I return, and why?

Because I've noticed something,
that my body, stretched and lost,
is tingling and electrical
from head to foot, vibrating,
and I see the room I am in,
yet my eyes are closed
and I cannot open them.

I look about and soon
I am surprised
because this is not my room.

Who changed the curtains,
so that they have ruffles?
Who carved designs into the
posts of the room divider?
Who put strange pictures

on the wall?

Whose room is this I am in?
Yet it is my room, different,
but similar too.
Perhaps, with my eyelids closed,
I see more than I know is there.

Recognizing You

You leapt into my life,
entered my room with a leap,
a bounding springing jumping sweep
and yet you walked normally.

I recognized you,
yet had not met you before.

My eyes saw a new person
but my heart mimicked your entrance,
and it knew who you were.

My mind wants to know who you are!

My heart screams greetings to you
as if eons had passed in waiting
longingly for your return,
and it is filled with happy tears.
My mind is puzzled.

I tell you about this
and you are frightened.

Poetry Doesn't Pay

Poetry doesn't pay, they say.

I hate the stuff.
I wouldn't write it
except that it fills a few
heavy moments and
refreshed my energy.

Nobody reads it,
and when they do
they don't understand it,
and when they do,
they can't share it,
and when they do,
people look at them funny.

A poet is a court jester
without a court,
a fool in a too serious world,
a fool with no money,
a fool with nobody laughing.

Clearly a bunch of crap,
this business of poetry.

Ants

Little ants know what to do.
They carry things and scurry.

Architects of miniature mines
they build and fortify their homes
and they journey far,
and find their way back home.

A message from the universe,
these little ants describe to us
the joy of community, of creativity,
of purpose, of fulfillment,
of grand design, of identity.
Yet I know less than they do.

Why is the message of the ants
so difficult to read?

Jack on the Mountain

I climbed the mountain peak and saw
a low horizon spreading far,
and my friend Jack sat at my feet
and saw loose rocks about.

Jack gathered rocks and piled them high,
and marked his presence on the peak,
and raised the peak to greater height,
and left a greater mountain there.

No record book was changed that day,
No one observed the number change,
Yet height was added to that peak
and Jack and I knew all about it.

A Face In the Clouds

The wide Texas sky is cluttered
with a congregation of clouds
from every family in the atmosphere.

I am absorbed in their wrangling,
their negotiations for new balance,
and am witness to their heated talks.

One party shouts for peace,
another, war,
and sparks begin to fly,
visible to me as flashing bolts.

And the argument begins,
shaking the skies with
thunderous harangue.

The sweat begins to pour out in sheets,
so vigorous are their attacks.

I am a quiet witness to all of this,
marvelling at this other-worldly spate,
caught up in its intensity,
when a Rembrandt face appears,
etched magnificently into the clouds,
smiling to me,
saying all will soon be resolved.

Sandwich

It is lunchtime and I see
that there is some lunch for me.

When I open up the sack,
there's a sandwich looking back.

Looking like one I prepared
several hours ago at home.

I recall now making it--
sliced tomato and some cheese,
meat and then the mayonnaise,
and I cut it into two
like a restauranteur might do,
bagged and put it in the sack,
carried it to work with me.

How it got here, what it is,
shouldn't pose a mystery.

And yet somehow something more
needs to be accounted for.

Donna Lena

Donna Lena, where are the West Indies?

Are they so far
the world was forced to toss us
across oceans and plains
so that we could meet?

Are they so far that time
was made to rush,
so that we could clearly see each other
Through race and age and stature?

Do they dream there
of soul-mates scattered in the wind,
who scramble to a common meeting place?

Are they in a sphere of mirth
where laughter is a magic password
and a secret way of knowing one another?

Do mothers there whisper
in their daughters' ears
of love awaiting in a magic land,
that when they grow and taste the world,
a love will show, and take command,
and make of life a rapture and a joy?

Have these West Indies given birth to you
for me?

Donna

Donna, do you love me?
Never let me know,
for I might take you for a fool,
and then where would you be?

Donna, do you trust me?
Never take a chance,
for I might pounce and hurt you,
and what a fool you'd be.

Donna, do you want me?
Never ask out loud,
for I may simply use you,
and you'd be left alone.

Donna, do I love you?
How easily I could.
I'd never take you for a fool,
for then a fool I'd be.

Donna, do I trust you?
I really cannot say.
But I will take the risk and learn
if then a fool I'd be.

Donna, do I want you?
I want you, yes and no.
But if I take you into me,
We'll never be alone.

For My Beloved Rebecca

strangled by life,
tortured and tossed,
lost in the maze of events,
grasping for threads and
gasping for breaths,
hopelessly clinging and
helplessly screaming,
trampled and broken,
we find inner strength.
like butterflies
we emerge, amazed.

we survive, astonished.
we see we are whole.
we can fly.

we fly to each other,
and the world vanishes;
we only are in the world.
we meet and explore.
afraid to be fools,
we question the miracle
and examine its fabric,
its weave.

the miracle pervades us,
our questions seem foolish,
and when we embrace,
the world vanishes;

our bliss is completed,
and only our toes
touch this world.

The WP Blues

My words, my words, are you okay?
The writer agonized again
For words of his had slipped away
and swum in cables' disarray
and entered swift a basic box
and flew around god who knows where
til they were sucked by cable two
and spat upon the amber screen.

Ah, there you are, but are you really?
I see you now but will you still be?
For what he sees is a mirage
and unrecorded it will be,
unless, until, he takes the risk
and sends his words out to the disk.

So off they go, their merry way,
the words acabling they do go,
and whiz around inside the box
til they are whizzed upon the disk.
My words, my words, are you okay?
I saved you but you went away.
Now I can't see you; are you there?
Watch the writer get gray hair.

Create

From consciousness I intend it.
My mind builds order around it.
And my body tends to the material reality.

I see my mind as my tool.
In no way does my mind share
in my existence.

And so I see my body also.

This is my creative process.
By operating this process
from consciousness
I have little to do
with its manifestations.

My tools are at work for me,
and I give them freedom.
My mind and my body
do the best they can.

I couldn't ask for more.

Done It All

One day I turned around
and realized
that I had done it all

And realized
that it was finally time
to meet the challenge
I had never faced
nor really dared to face

It was all that remained undone
There was nothing else to do
And I became a man of God

Zorba's Dance

Money, war and nature
Are leading us to Hell.
Funny we don't see it;
Maybe just as well.

Insanity is rampant,
Hiding in the books;
Profanity's malignant
Because of hero crooks.

We walk the daily walk,
We see but look askance;
Our choice is not to balk;
Just join in Zorba's dance.

Mother Goose Took a Shit

Hey, diddle, diddle, the cat and the fiddle,
The cow took a shit.
The little dog laughed to see such sport,
And the dish took a shit.

Humpty Dumpty sat on a wall.
Humpty Dumpty took a shit
All the king's horses took a shit
and all the king's men took a shit.

Diddle, diddle, dumpling,
my son, John, took a shit

Hickory, dickory, dock,
The mouse took a shit.

This little piggy went to market,
This little piggy stayed home,
This little piggy had roast beef,
This little piggy had none,
And this little piggy took a shit.

Itsy bitsy spider climbed up the water spout;
Down came the rain and washed the spider out;
Out came the sun and dried up all the rain;
And the itsy bitsy spider took a shit.

www.ingramcontent.com/pod-product-compliance
Lightning Source LLC
LaVergne TN
LVHW051839080426
835512LV00018B/2963